Marie de Quatrebarbes

The Vitals

translated from French by Aiden Farrell

 WORLD POETRY

The Vitals by Marie de Quatrebarbes
Copyright © P.O.L Éditeur, 2021
English translation copyright © Aiden Farrell, 2025

Originally published as *Les vivres* (Paris: P.O.L, 2021)

First Edition, First Printing, 2025
ISBN 978-1-954218-32-1

World Poetry Books
New York, NY
worldpoetrybooks.com

Available to the trade through Asterism Books
Distributed in the UK and Europe by Turnaround Publisher Services
Subscriptions and standing orders available directly from the publisher

Library of Congress Control Number: 2025930687

Cover design by Andrew Bourne
Typesetting by Don't Look Now
Printed in Lithuania by BALTO Print

This work received support for excellence in publication and translation from Albertine Translation, a program created by Villa Albertine and funded by Albertine Foundation. Additional funding was provided by Centre national du livre: CNL.

World Poetry Books is a 501(c)(3) nonprofit and charitable organization founded in 2017 in New York City, affiliated with the Humanities Institute and the Translation Program at the University of Connecticut (Storrs), and a member of the Community of Literary Magazines and Presses (CLMP).

World Poetry's publications and programs are made possible with funding from the Poetry Foundation and the New York State Council on the Arts, as well as generous support from individual donors and subscribers.

The Vitals

July 11
August 37
September 49
October 73
November 93
December 119

Translator's Afterword 135
Acknowledgments 141

Les vivres

The Vitals

VIE : « Je serai lointaine,
mais je ne t'abandonnerai pas. »

Andrea Zanzotto, *Phosphènes*

LIFE: "I'll be far away,
but I will not abandon you."

    Andrea Zanzotto, *Fosfeni*

Juillet

July

1er.

En rangeant des affaires, j'ai reconnu le regard de son chien dans celui de Clint Eastwood. C'était une tasse en porcelaine japonaise découpée, dans la tasse japonaise qui. Les enfants furent les premiers. Ensuite, il y eut une perruche à laquelle elle disait : il est tard, rentre chez toi. Elle avait peur quand j'étais seule et que la nuit tombait. Le mois qui précède, elle se souvient que je l'ai appelée un soir, dans le parc désert. Les lumières clignotaient et j'étais ivre. Lorsque s'effondre le meuble dans lequel elle range les tasses japonaises offertes par mémé, précieusement je conserve les larmes où je les imagine.

1st.

As I was putting things away, I recognized her dog's gaze in Clint Eastwood's. It was a cut-out Japanese porcelain teacup in the Japanese teacup that. The children were the first. Next, there was a parakeet to whom she said: it's late, go home. She was afraid when I was alone and night was falling. The month before, she remembers that I called her from the deserted park one evening. The lights flickered and I was drunk. When the cabinet in which she arranges the Japanese teacups Grandma gave her collapses, I keep the tears in which I imagine them preciously.

2.

À la voir en cette fin d'après-midi, la totalité, la voir, elle s'est arrêtée devant l'inscription qui la donnait pour super, mémoriale, excellente. Dehors, la fumée d'un champignon improvise la fumée qui monte d'une étagère. Je ne peux dire si elle fut brève, ou bien s'échappant d'un plan extrême de netteté. À la voir échappée, le mouvement fut. À la fois, c'est la nuit. Les pleurs se tiennent en équilibre au-dessus du drap vertical. Les cils battent la fumée à la recherche d'un conflit plus extérieur. Constante est un nombre incalculable de fois. Je ne dis pas qu'ils constatent la disparition, je dis qu'ils ne sont pas sûrs de la voir.

2.

To see her at the end of that afternoon—the totality, to see her—she stopped in front of an inscription that made her out to be the best, memorable, excellent. Outside, the smoke of a mushroom becomes the smoke rising from a shelf. I can't say if she was brief or escaping an extreme plan of clarity. Seeing her escape, the movement was. At once, it's night. Tears hang in equilibrium above a vertical sheet. Eyelashes bat at smoke in search of a more exterior conflict. Constant is an incalculable number of times. I'm not saying they constitute disappearance—I'm saying they're not sure they see her.

3.

Couper les cheveux de grand-mère avec des ciseaux de couture se révéla fort simple, en dépit des ciseaux qui n'étaient pas faits pour cela. De la lingerie démontée point par point, je comptais les ronds aux noms effacés. Le livre, multiplement annoté, les phrases dans les marges reprennent les marges du texte. Je crois qu'elle parlait d'une poupée dont le corps était comme. *Momwey*, c'est l'objet de mon trouble. Avec lui je m'imagine un compagnon qui me rapproche d'autres noms que lui-même.

3.

Cutting grandma's hair with sewing scissors turned out to be easy despite using scissors made for something else. From lingerie dismantled piece by piece, I counted the circles of erased names. The book, variously annotated, marginalia reclaiming the margins. I think she was describing a doll the body resembled. *Mom-mee* is the object of my confusion. With him, I fancy myself a companion that brings me closer to names other than himself.

4.

J'aimerais écrire des phrases emboîtées comme des poupées russes. Loger dans leur ventre de bois creux un secret peut préserver : une rose est dans une rose, une abeille dans une abeille. J'ai rêvé qu'on t'avait monté la tête à l'envers, si bien qu'il fallait te tenir l'épaule pour que tu ne tombes pas, la tête renversée. Celui qui ne dit rien, là-bas, ton visage parle pour lui. Maintenant que je te regarde j'ai l'impression que quelqu'un court sur ta coiffure.

4.

I'd like to write sentences that contain each other like Russian dolls. A secret could persist, lodged in their hollow wooden stomachs: a rose is in a rose, a bee in a bee. I dreamt that we mounted your head upside down, such that you had to hold on to your shoulders to stop from falling, your head inverted. That one who isn't saying anything, over there, your face speaks for him. Now that I'm looking at you, it seems like someone's running across your haircut.

5.

On s'habitue aux écritures penchées où il n'y a plus d'enfants, lorsqu'ils sont devenus grands et leurs yeux reculent dans le visage. Tu parles d'une image aux chaussettes tirebouchonnées. La faïence n'a pas de pli. Le corps est celui des étapes précédentes, avec le rire qui fut le son qu'elle produisit. Il y a le scandale d'une possession, le choc invité à ma table, puis une autre partie commence. Nous nous occuperons du squelette, petit. Je ne suis plus celle que j'étais comme je fus l'enfant d'une seule fois. La ronde des chaises, assorties, vides, sur lesquelles le programme n'assoit rien, refait la disparition dont nous tenons les premiers rôles.

5.

One gets used to slanted writing in which there are no longer children, not once they've grown up and their eyes have sunk. You're talking about an image of corkscrewed socks. Ceramics have no creases. The body is that of previous states, laughter being the sound she produced. There's the scandal of a possession, shock invited to my table, then another act begins. We'll busy ourselves with the skeleton, little one. I'm no longer the one I was as I was the child of a single time. The ring of chairs, various, empty, on which the program bases nothing, repeats the disappearance in which we play the leading roles.

6.

Ce visage qui fut le mien, frotté très fort au mustela, contient la somme des visages collés. Et le gâteau d'un moment revient dans son extase, avec les récipients troués, je les versais, je les versais. Tu t'improvises, m'inventes une joie. Si ce courage est le mien et que tu serres ma main fort, la couleur s'approche de plusieurs reflets à la fois. Je forme avec la bouche le mot de quelque chose. Je me dé-remémore.

6.

This face that was mine, with moisturizer thoroughly rubbed in, contains the sum of glued faces. And the cake of a moment returns in ecstasy, its vessels pierced—I emptied them, I emptied them. You improvise yourself, create joy for me. If this courage is my own and you hold my hand tight, then color approaches several reflections at once. I form a word for something with my mouth. I disremember myself.

7.

Si souvent qu'ils s'ennuient les enfants devraient dire : nous sommes les figurants d'un parage de fiction. Nous nous pré-promenons. Allons-y gaiement, allons-y, ne refaisons pas les fous. J'ai reçu la bande audio d'un copain, à la fois proche et ses gestes sont les miens quand, aux miens, je m'accorde à ce que nous avons de commun. Si souvent qu'ils s'ennuient les enfants devraient dire : nous sommes les figurants d'un parage de fiction.

7.

So often are they bored that the children ought to say: we're extras in a fictional zone. We go for a pre-walk. Let's go, gladly now, here we go, don't go crazy this time. I received the tape recording from a friend—we're similar. His gestures are mine when, with mine, I tune myself to what we have in common. So often are they bored that the children ought to say: we're extras in a fictional zone.

8.

Assez de vie pour décider d'une fois autre. Le cordon de la salle de bains au bord du récipient maintient le chien dans son état initial. Ensuite les animaux disent oui aux enfants de conserve. Ce que les armoires connaissent de nos jouets, quand ils ont rejoint la colonie. Suit le plan où l'on regarde, il y a plusieurs fois la même main à la pliure. Pourtant l'espace n'aperçoit pas de l'autre côté comme la poupée se tient et l'enfant croît. Entre ici et la chaise assez vide, suffisamment lui revient pour céder une fois autre.

8.

Enough life to decide at another time. The bathroom cord at the edge of the vessel keeps the dog in its initial state. Next, the animals say yes to the canned children. What the wardrobes know about our toys, when they rejoined the colony. Follow our plan to watch, the same hand is at the fold several times. Yet the space apprehends the other side neither the way the doll holds itself nor as the child develops. Enough comes back to him between here and the rather empty chair for him to surrender again.

13.

Les enfants actés se préparent familièrement à verser dans l'acte de violence. Par la vitrine des tasses brisées, l'attention ne faiblit pas. Manquée se présente comme une image juste, à l'intersection de celles, des images ou des actes, qui sont des enfants. Assez vivement, les petits pois sont blancs, leur solitude est un recoin dont l'œil sait quelque chose. À quoi bon chercher des prétextes, quand déplacer la position ne résout rien ? Mes chaussures sont des classements qui font la course.

13.

The re-enacted children casually prepare to transition into acts of violence. By the window of shattered cups, caution doesn't waver. Missed is presented as a fair picture at the intersection of those—pictures or acts—that are children. Quickly, the peas are white. Their solitude is a recess of which an eye knows a thing or two. Why find excuses when changing positions resolves nothing? My shoes are rankings. They race around the track.

19.

L'enfance vivait dans les toilettes d'une maison plus petite que la plupart des maisons. Sur la tapisserie des formes récitaient des extraits du dictionnaire que je prenais pour des images. Si je pense aux larmes qui suivirent les bris et fracas : comment savoir quand c'est son tour de pleurer ? Certainement qu'un dernier souffle signala qu'elle était décidée, alors qu'aucune autre sortie ne communiquait avec la chambre. À la voir je me suis dit : son œil est d'or et sa bouche un secret.

19.

Childhood lived in the bathrooms of a house smaller than most houses. On the tapestry shapes recited dictionary entries I took for images. If I think of the tears that followed the breaks and crashes: how to know when it's one's turn to cry? Surely the last breath meant she was resolute as no other exit connected with the room. On seeing her I said to myself: her eye is of gold and her mouth a secret.

26.

On l'habilla d'une robe qui lui allait. On coiffa ses cheveux que j'avais coupés. Puis l'enfant quitta sa cage et s'excusa d'un oubli. Je me promène sans doute dans cet oubli-là. J'entends sa voix quand je regarde, par hasard, du côté où elle se trouve. Parfois je ris sans le savoir.

26.

We put her in a dress that flattered her. We styled her hair, which I had cut. Then the child left her cage and apologized for the oversight. I'm probably walking in that oversight. I hear her voice when I look, absent-mindedly, to the side where she is. Sometimes I laugh without knowing.

27.

Par emboîtements légers, je me présente aux étapes d'une jeunesse fictive. Le regard n'a pas de bras pour désigner ce qui arrive dépend de beaucoup. Puis c'est le col, déplaçant la bretelle, qui indique une direction que la poupée suit. De la disparition, je conserve les angles seulement. Depuis qu'une alarme fut posée, elle parlait de l'intérieur de son ventre. Je ne me souviens pas d'un autre temps qu'il y ait eu, mais la manière dont elle me voit constate qu'en fin de compte je n'y suis plus. Je ne suis pas là lorsqu'elle me quitte. Je dors dans un train. Je ne suis pas bien grande. Comme il est dangereux, parfois, de contempler là où la face est réversible : il faut conjurer ces moments-là, va savoir, s'ils existent.

27.

I present myself in the phases of a fictional youth with neatly woven threads. A gaze has no arms to express that what happens depends on a lot. Then it's the collar, displacing suspenders that point in the direction a doll follows. I keep only the angles from the disappearance. After an alarm had been raised, she spoke from inside her stomach. I don't remember if there had been another time but based on my calculations the way she looks at me confirms that I'm no longer there. I'm no longer there when she leaves me. I sleep on a train. I'm not that big. It's dangerous, you know, sometimes, to contemplate, here, where a face is reversible: one must fend off these moments perhaps, if they exist.

Août

August

1er.

Les bruits éclatent jusqu'aux parois. Mon cœur se jette à ma tête d'une force contagieuse. Puis le petit globe osseux qui contient mes pensées et des éclats de verre s'ouvre, c'est ainsi. Quelqu'un traverse la pièce et tu as l'impression d'être toi-même ce petit globe. Ce n'est pas vrai qu'ils parlent, les murs, des bruits, des gestes et du tissu posé là inexplicablement. À l'entendre, c'est toi qui te déchires. Comment expliquer qu'il te paraisse d'une telle innocence ?

1st.

Noises burst at the walls. My heart rushes to my head with a contagious force. Then the little globe of bone that contains my thoughts and shattered glass opens, and that's that. Someone crosses the room and you get the impression that the little globe is you. It isn't true that they speak, the walls, noises, gestures and tissue left here without explanation. To hear it, it's you ripping yourself up. How to explain that to you it seems so innocent?

2.

Nous avons vu les rats et maintenant nous nous tutoyons. La tête et la barbe ont l'air rouges sur fond d'air. Quelqu'un se lève et c'est ça, déjà, les poings sur la table. Sténographie du poème jeté vite, avec tendresse. Gros plan sur le visage lorsqu'il chante. Saccades dans une forêt de formes. Ici on invente une bâche pour recouvrir. La peur de voir réapparaître. Le poing en rapprochement progressif. Je ne fais que répéter : les parapluies dont l'ombre jette sur le pont la masse des gens et le filet noir. C'est dans ce monde que je vis.

2.

We saw the rats and now we're on a first-name basis. Both the head and beard have an air of red on a background of air. Someone gets up, fists on the table, and that's that, in itself. The poem in shorthand jotted quickly, with tenderness. Close-up of face when singing. Spasms in a forest of forms. Here we invent a tarpaulin to cover over. The fear to see reappear. The fist in progressive approach. I'm only repeating: the umbrellas whose shadow falls on the mass of people on the bridge and the black net. I live in this world.

3.

D'approche plus délicate, intime, nous nous tutoyons mais qui sommes-nous ? Peut-on voir plus précisément le visage penché sur l'objectif ? Et lorsqu'ils débarquent les vivres on compte les images, comment elles nous apparurent, dans leur brièveté, plus que jamais tenues dans une correspondance étroite. Je ne vais rien changer de toi. Elle dit : le sablier est la chose la plus triste qu'il m'ait été donné de voir. Tout le monde dit : le sablier est la chose la plus triste. Je ne fais que répéter. Cet instant précis.

3.

We're on a first-name basis, coming from a more delicate, intimate place, but who are we? Are we able to see the face hanging from the objective more precisely? And when they unload the vitals we count the images, the way they appear to us, in their brevity, more than ever held in close correspondence. I won't change anything about you. She says: an hourglass was the saddest thing he had given me to see. Everyone says: hourglasses are the saddest things. I'm only repeating. This precise instant.

4.

Elle monte, un carton chargé dans les bras. Dans l'élan qui ne veut pas commencer. Si vous lisez ceci. Ce n'est pas un hasard si quelques lignes évasives s'effacent. Si vous lisez encore. Rien ne semble plus vaste à cet instant que le carton qu'elle porte dans ses bras. Un seul élément flotte. Le cœur, entravé par la crainte. Elle se confond dans un moment de honte. Les grèves, les tempêtes, le cri porté hors. Voilà, dit-elle, c'est l'univers. La vague, c'est sa faiblesse. Elle enregistre tout ce qu'elle dit.

4.

She climbs, an overfilled box in her arms. Within an impulse that doesn't want to begin. If you read this. It's not a coincidence that a few evasive lines erase themselves. If you're still reading. Right now, nothing seems as vast as the box she carries. One single element floats. The heart, fettered by doubt. She's confounded in a moment of shame. Shores, storms, the scream carried out. Voilà, she says, the universe. The wave. It's her weakness. She documents everything she says.

5.

Il y a le geste comme une occasion de renaître. Au milieu du tumulte et des brumes, les corps amoncelés. On a vu des mains où il y avait du sang. On était des fumées dans la nuit. On regarde quelque chose de rouge qu'on a sous les ongles. On ne se souvient plus du moment. On danse sur le pont quand personne ne regarde. Sur l'eau il y a des fuyards. Nous sommes des fuyards. Ça ressemble à un théâtre de cire. Je me sens plus vieille que le groupe des plus vieilles femmes. Avec une fausse barbe on aura du soleil en novembre. Pour éclairer le ciel il faut couper l'électricité de la ville. Ça ne se fera pas du jour au lend'main. La main frappe le rebord de ce que je ne dis pas. Je me répète. Seulement par souci d'exactitude.

5.

There's gesture as an opportunity to be reborn. In the middle of the tumult and city haze, accumulated bodies. We saw hands with blood on them. We were smoke in the night. We examine something red under our nails. We forget the moment. We dance on the bridge when no one's looking. There are fugitives on the water. We're fugitives. It's like a theater of wax. I feel older than the group of older women. With a fake beard we'll have some sun in November. To illuminate the sky the town's electricity must be cut. It won't happen overnight. A hand smacks the rim of what I don't say. I repeat myself. Only for the sake of accuracy.

Septembre

September

1er.

Signes sans référent : fiction-faunes. Fugacités rendues d'après la guerre. Un signe est une fête qu'elle regarde depuis la mort. Ce peut-il être, un de ces jours terrestres, que se produise la disparition hâtive d'un lien ? Car, pour être, magique est incertain. Présente un drame à l'incomplétude abstr. d'une img. sûre. Seulement peut-elle, pour être, provoquer incert. destin ?

1st.

Signs without referent: fauna-fiction. Fugacities rendered post-war. A sign is a party she watches from death. Can it be, one of these terrestrial days, which produce the hurried disappearance of a connection? For, to exist, magic is uncertain. Puts on a drama of the abst. incompletion of a certain img. To exist, can it alone provoke uncert. fate?

2.

On ne ruse pas avec elle. Et si elle tombe, on la confie à des abeilles. La tête en avant, les cornes, le buste. Concours d'élégance. Façon de dire : circonstances. Ici, tout est gratuité. La subtilité vient du propos. Une fiction s'achemine : l'après-midi, les enfants... fiction à laquelle on ne peut répondre qu'en hochant la tête, lorsqu'une idée vague, très vague, vaporeuse même, vient nous l'arracher. Elle tourne, la tête, toujours, dans le sens du vent.

2.

We don't trick her. And if she falls, we entrust her to the bees. Head forward, horns, bust. An elegance pageant. Figure of speech: circumstances. Everything is free here. Subtlety comes from the word. A fiction advances: the afternoon, the children… fiction to which one can only respond with a nod when a vague idea, a very vague idea, vaporous even, comes to snatch it away. She turns. Her head, always, in the direction of the wind.

3.

Ce qui se mange : les vivres. Le visage à ce titre, la fin de l'année. Les marais vides, leur eau saumâtre, irréductiblement jaune. Quand je dis « on » (des pommes), le petit canard boiteux, celui qu'on a mis dans la poche de l'enfant, je veux dire « lui » se sauve (ce n'est pas lui). Sorte d'extase, délire de possession, le reflet devant l'œil grossi à la loupe, la perte de l'image. Code : passant du vert au paysage. Variante : elle est ce vieux garçon à la bouche bleue.

3.

What is eaten: the vitals. The face as such, the end of the year. Empty swamps, their water brackish, irreducibly yellow. When I say "we" (apples)—the little lame duck, the one we put in the child's pocket—I mean "he" saves himself (it isn't him). A sort of ecstasy, delusion of ownership—the reflection in front of an eye grows in the magnifying glass—loss of the image. Code: passing from green to landscape. Variant: she's that old boy with the blue mouth.

4.

Bouche plate (option de retrait). Par bouche s'entend : poreuse. Dans le déploiement du vent : fenêtre, son hochement imbibé. Focale : adoration-réclusion. La fonction dépolie d'un usage.

4.

Flat mouth (option to withdraw). Heard with mouth: porous. In the implementation of wind: window—its soaked nod. Focal: reclusion-adoration. The frozen function of a use.

5.

Ce vide : ma peau l'a démontré. On croit naître, dit-on, des figures noires de monde, d'abstraites nudités qui se tiennent dans une fixité compromise. Elles appellent cela : des rêves. Et nous les caressons. Nos mains cherchent leurs yeux, c'est ce que l'on fait avec les choses (elles ne sont pas des choses). Il fait souvent froid, l'éclat, celui-là, le même égosillement.

5.

This void: my skin illustrated it. We believe we are born, they say, from swarms of bodies, abstract nudities held in compromised steadiness. They call it: dreams. And we caress them. Our hands reach for their eyes. It's how we treat things (they are not things). The rupture is often cold, this one, the same scream.

6.

Hier un nuage s'est abattu sur la ville. Ma fenêtre a fait au monde une fine surface et je me suis demandé : où sont les lits ? Je suis couverte des pelures extérieures d'un oignon. Ma bouche in situ : accélération narrative. Nous trouvons le temps à l'endroit où nous l'avons laissé, dans les pots d'écrevisses. De l'intérieur, cette nuit, la bibliothèque a brûlé et les livres ont été dévorés par les flammes. Dire encore : pleureuses ont-elles un singulier ?

6.

Yesterday a cloud descended on the city. My window turned the world into a thin surface and I wondered: where are the beds? I'm covered in an onion's outermost skin. My mouth in situ: narrative acceleration. We find time in the same place we left it—in the pots of crayfish. Inside, tonight, the library burned down and the books were devoured by flames. Say again: do mourners have a singular?

11.

Une fiction danse à travers lui, qui n'est pas son corps ou un corps second qui n'a pas ses bras, ses jambes. À peine plus grand, le vêtement est premier (l'autre à l'intérieur). Évocation d'une musique peut-être faite des parcelles de son corps à lui, ou bien des nœuds d'un corps à sa mesure. Décision : des plages s'étendent à travers lui. Ligatures : subterfuge d'une hésitation résolue. Je ne lis pas ces mots, la trame d'un fait. Si vous êtes face à un frêne, il dira que vous êtes visage. D'après votre visage, vous refrénez votre désir.

11.

A fiction dances through him, which is neither his body nor a second body without his arms, his legs. Barely larger, the garment comes first (the other inside). Evocation of a music made of fragments of his own body, maybe, or pieces of a body around the size of his. Decision: beaches extend across him. Ligatures: the subterfuge of a resolute hesitation. I don't read these words—the plot of a fact. If you face an ash tree it will say that you are face. Looking at your face, you suppress your desire.

17.

Bras (ponctuations) : m'en tombent. Manières & fautes, à enjamber, prêtent au nom l'extinction d'une espèce. Dans le livre, tombées par accident, les différences ôtent au présage sa fuite. Surface : revêtement blanc. Froid dans le dos à envisager cet empressement. Note : calcaire. Des essaims touchent le texte où la pensée brûle.

17.

Eyes (punctuations): they fail me. Methods & faults—to step over—"lend the extinction of a species to the name. In the book, fallen to the floor by accident, differences strip an omen of its escape. Surface: white layer. Shivers down my spine to envision such vigor. Note: limestone. Swarms touch the text where thought burns.

24.

Excepte-moi, frêne, croyant venu peut-être le revêtement de laine, plonge le vert et les noyaux. Se peut-il que lui-même soit abs. ext. air ? Nous n'irons plus au bois. Qu'à cela ne tienne, une abs. tenue pour : son ombrage. Mon pouvoir est mon lieu. Hors d'usage, les rites familiers, et tout ce qui se meut : principes.

24.

Exclude me, ash tree, believing that perhaps the protective layer of wool arrived—plunge of green and the fruit's pit. Can it be that he, himself, is abs. ext. air? We won't go to the woods anymore. Never mind, an abs. held for: his shade. My power is my place. Out of service, the familiar rites and everything that moves: principles.

25.

Trombes. Les yeux déclenchent : la charge. Le parc est balbutiant. Planté là, courant comme des jambes, Bruegel et son linge. Les enfants galiciens, ceux qui ont été mis à la porte. Comète rouge. Forêt où les glaciations commencent. La photographie d'un point. Chute : d'un cheval embusqué. Rose : mythe. Bleu : phonème. Gestes : des fumées qu'on ralentit.

25.

Waterspouts. Eyes trigger: the charge. The park is babbling. Bruegel and his laundry, planted here, running like a pair of legs. Galician children, the ones who were kicked out. Red comet. The forest in which glaciations begin. The photography of a point. Downfall: of a horse lying in wait. Pink: myth. Blue: phoneme. Gestures: smoke we slow down.

26.

Les bêtes sont bl. de visage et de nom. Une lampe fond dans l'ombre. Il y a un chien seul dans la rue. Il y a des bêtes au visage bl. Après, il y a la solitude qui les contient. Cent caresses plus tard, c'est toujours le même bl. Demain, je cours après les nids, les feuilles, je frappe les murs absents. Parfois l'empereur souffre de mélancolie. Enfance : la même étendue d'eau.

26.

The animals are bl. of face and name. A lamp melts in the dark. There is a dog alone in the street. There are animals who have bl. faces. Afterward, solitude contains them. One hundred caresses later, it's still the same bl. Tomorrow, I run after nests, leaves, I hit the absent walls. Sometimes the emperor suffers melancholy. Childhood: the same body of water.

Octobre

October

1er.

Depuis la parcelle sur pilotis où je passe des vacances sans nervures, je frappe les lettres au parcours d'une rue, facile. Mains pelisses, mains maraudes, comme s'il fallait se tenir à distance. Puis les champs s'interrompent. L'enfance bouge d'un plan. Point de touche où je rêve. Aux doutes, les habitudes font des bouts de ficelle et les pages de romans, sitôt elles tombent, je leur fausse compagnie.

1st.

From the house on stilts where I spend vacations without venation, I hit the letters along a street—easy. Fur-lined hands, marauding hands, as if needing to keep one's distance. Then the fields break off. Childhood shifts planes. Point of contact where I dream. Habits use bits of thread and the pages of novels to make doubts. No sooner they fall. I ran out on them.

2.

J'ai perdu mon poudrier gris : promesse. Il y a des lieux plus loin que les lieux. Passées au crible d'une ressemblance, il y a d'insignes réalités, des paysages que même le paysage ne voit pas. Nous habitons de logiques parcelles, des chantiers malaisés qu'on croirait sous attente. Et si ton amie tombe, la mort, faisant mine d'attraper, le manche, même si rarement le temps d'un rapport autorise, la distance, c'est donné pour un donnant. Le transport est gratuit, pas l'effort.

2.

I lost my gray powder compact: promise. There are locations beyond locations. Carefully examined for a likeness, there are symbolic realities, landscapes even the landscape doesn't see. We inhabit logical plots of land, uneasy construction sites we presume are waiting. And if your friend falls, death, pretending to catch, the handle, even if the time for a report seldom allows, the distance, it is given to a giving. The transportation is free, not the effort.

3.

Des phrases accidentées du couple pain/plan, des arguments comme disent les enfants, d'un front nu : va, selon. J'ai appris qu'ici un paysage s'est donné pour le vivre des ordres très différents, s'unissant. Il y a des pensées qui s'accrochent et des fleurs aux délicats jabots. Les images et les mots sont en fait irréconciliables. Ils se juxtaposent au faire-semblant et laissent s'égratigner l'air. On calcule à peine le mouvement que permet l'accentuation. Pour rapporter les choses à leur réalité, la seule, depuis le souffle que fut le paysage, à défaut du mouvement le combat est libre.

3.

The damaged sentences of the bread/blueprint partnership. Arguments, as the children like to say with a nude forehead: go, depending on. I learned that here a landscape has given itself alternative rules to live by, unifying. There are thoughts that stick and flowers of delicate frills. Images and words are in fact irreconcilable. Make-believe juxtaposes them and they let the air scratch. We just about calculate the movement the emphasis permits. To bring things back to their reality, the one and only, since the breath that was the landscape, combat is free in the absence of movement.

4.

C'est un paysage en mouvement, tel qu'à quelque point où l'on regarde, il est beau. Alors je monte le dialogue d'un cran. Les bougies fument sur leur cône, manifestement. Ma vision se défait. J'ai vu, avant les yeux, des mers agitées. J'ai remisé mes souliers aux grands pieds. J'ai dormi dans mon souci. J'ai nagé avant nager. J'ai pressé la pulpe et j'ai crié. J'ai cru qu'elle m'appelait.

4.

It's a landscape in motion, such that wherever you look, it's beautiful. So I turn the dialogue up a notch. The candles smoke on their cone, manifestly. My vision fades. I saw rough seas before eyes. I put away my oversized shoes. I slept in my worry. I swam before swimming. I pressed the pulp and I screamed. I thought she had called me.

5.

C'est une grande faiblesse d'âme. Remets-toi au monde, s'il te plaît. Promets-moi de commencer, à nouveau. Il faut avoir ce qu'il faut, de quoi faire son omelette. La liste d'un seul ingrédient. Recette indemne, tes grogs étaient constants : un jaune blanc, du lait rouge, un peu de rhum-espace. Qu'est-ce que c'est d'être ? C'est l'hiver et ça crie des chambres d'enfants. Ici, on joue bas. Ce fond de toi parle d'un tout petit fond brumeux, du bleu posé à l'angle, une fenêtre, des sardines. Toujours plus éloignées, ou l'ultra-évidence où nous étions, portées l'une vers l'autre, d'une même longueur d'âme.

5.

It's a great weakness of the soul. Return yourself to the world, please. Promise me you'll begin, anew. One must have what one must have, enough to make an omelet. The list of a single ingredient. Unharmed recipe. Your grogs were constant: a white yellow, red milk, a dash of space-rum. What is it to be? It is winter and there are screams from the children's rooms. Here, we play down low. Your depth suggests a shallow, foggy depth, blue positioned at an angle, a window, sardines. Always more drawn out—or the ultra-evidence where we were, one carried toward the other—than the wavelength of the soul.

6.

Remets-toi au monde et plante-toi dans le décor, à nouveau. Il est temps, nous sortirons comme des grandes. Ténu, c'est vivant. On se parle des couleurs et tu pars toi, à vitesse croissante. Au croisement de j'ai peur, il est dit que j'ai peur. Mes doigts collent à la minute précédente, la première minute d'un seul jour. Étions-nous courageux de commencer ? D'une seule touche, remets-toi. Terre rouge de mes souliers blessés, terre de cauchemars. Au marché de ma rencontre, j'ai tout de suite su. Les bougies fument sur leur cône, manifestement. Là où le poème n'a de sens, conception voilée, durée pulsée d'avant la pente.

6.

Return to the world and plant yourself in the scenery, anew. It's time, we'll exit like grown-ups. It's alive, tenuous. We talk about colors and you, you get up and leave, with increasing speed. At the intersection of I'm scared, it is said that I'm scared. My fingers stick to the preceding minute, the first minute of a single day. Were we brave to begin? With one touch, recover. Red earth of my wounded shoes, earth of nightmares. At the market where we met, I immediately knew. The candles smoke on their cone manifestly. Here where the poem has no sense, veiled conception, duration pulsing ahead of the slope.

7.

Je suis descendue au niveau de ma peur, et tandis qu'elle rebrousse chemin, avec les bêtes, on revient vers les lumières qui sont cassées ou brillent peu. Dessein inchangé, un même assemblage de laine et de papier collant au sol comme poussière, le petit cadran s'est brisé. Que savons-nous d'eux lorsqu'ils nous atteignent ? Les questions sont visuelles, des arguments qui retournent aux collines avec les cailloux roulant du sol aux poches, défonçant les doublures. La lumière s'est peut-être ajustée à ce qu'elle peut voir. Qu'en serait-il du chant sans le vent ?

7.

I stooped to the level of my fear, and as she retraced her steps with the animals, we returned to the variously broken and fading lights. Unaltered design, the same assemblage of wool and paper stuck to the ground like dust, the little watch face broke. What do we know about them when they reach us? Questions are visual, arguments that churn in the hills with pebbles rolling from the ground into pockets, wearing down the inner lining. The light may have adjusted to what she can see. What of song without wind?

8.

Elle disait rouges, les feintes, les jours où tout est à l'envers. Les poumons sont des pièces où l'orchestre est caché. Les questions : visuelles. D'un bras la touche, ostensible, le lait rouge de l'enfance. Des circonstances, pour que le sens diminue dans la durée, et autour tourne la tempête. Les nuits incertaines s'enchaînent aux nuits continues. Je pense en mouvement. Il y a le feu qui sèche mes joues et tout ce qui était connu se dispense. Remets-toi.

8.

She said red, pretenses, days where everything is upside down. Lungs are rooms in which the orchestra is hidden. Questions: visuals. Touches the red milk of childhood, ostensibly, with one arm. Circumstances so that sense diminishes inside duration. The storm circles it. Hesitant nights follow continuous nights. I think in motion. There's the fire drying my cheeks and all that was known is spared. Return yourself.

9.

Bientôt nous serons seules, comme des grandes. Nous nous pendrons des baisers, des buissons, de recul. Ténu, c'est vivant. Alors, on se parle des couleurs, elles sont là, toutes en-là, et tu pars, toi, à vitesse croissante. Au croisement de j'ai peur, il est dit que j'ai peur. Mes doigts collent à la minute précédente. Remets-toi dans le sable, d'une seule touche, en enfance. Terre rouge de mes souliers blessés, terre de cauchemars. Au marché de ma rencontre, j'ai tout de suite su. Elle disait rouges, les feintes, les jours où tout est à l'envers. Je ne te croyais de ce monde, astreinte, où je suis descendue.

9.

Soon we'll be alone, like grown-ups. We'll suspend ourselves from kisses, from bushes, from hindsight. Tenuous, life is. So, we talk about colors. They're there, all there, and you leave, you, with increasing speed. At the intersection of I'm scared, it is said that I'm scared. My fingers stick to the preceding minute. Return yourself to the sand with one touch, in childhood. Red earth of my wounded shoes, earth of nightmares. At the market where we met, I knew immediately. She said red, pretenses, days where everything is upside down. I didn't believe you were of this world, on call, to which I descended.

Novembre

November

1er.

Au bord parfois très pentu où je me penche, je m'en vais m'aligner sur un espoir plus grand. Ajuster ce qu'il faut voir peut retirer à tout moment ce que le bras donne, la main le reprend. Le jour de son départ, l'œil voulait simplement faire le point. Prolongeant cet état où la main refait le trajet de point fixe, ici plonge en avant un point où visiblement se précise. Au bord parfois très pentu où je me penche, je m'en vais m'aligner sur un espoir.

1st.

At the occasionally very steep edge on which I lean, I'm going to align myself with higher hopes. Adjusting what must be seen can at any moment remove what an arm gives. The hand reclaims it. The day of his departure—the eye simply wanted to take stock. Here a point dives forward where it becomes visibly clearer, prolonging the state where a hand repeats the trajectory of a fixed point. At the occasionally very steep edge on which I lean, I'm going to align myself with a hope.

6.

Si courir est à courir, maintenant la main veut. Si courir est à maintenant ce que maintenant veut la main, et si la main reprend la main, la main reste en la main. Je ne sais pas si demain nous aurons à tous les coups les chances, une fois dit nous aurons. Je ne sais pas si demain nous aurons le courage de dire nous, une fois dit nous aurons. Mais si nos vivres sont suffisants, il est certain que nous aurons tout ce qu'il faut nous appartient. Et si les moyens nous manquent, une fois dit nous aurons, si les moyens nous manquent il est certain que nous manquerons au manque.

6.

If running is to run, now the hand wants it. If running is right now what the hand now wants, and if the hand reclaims the hand, the hand stays in the hand. I don't know if we'll have any luck tomorrow, once said we will. I don't know if we'll have the confidence to say us, once said we will. But if our vitals suffice, it's certain that we'll have everything we need that belongs to us. And if we don't have the means—once it's said, we will—and if we don't have the means, it's certain that we'll be missing what's lacking.

12.

Sur le chemin de la fac, je m'allonge. Je m'allonge dans l'herbe, je m'allonge et l'herbe me tend les pieds, les mains, je m'allonge, je me baisse et mon regard devient ce qu'il est. Je m'allonge et mon regard devient ce qu'il est à la fois ce qu'il était. Je me penche sur l'herbe et je m'allonge, je me baisse et je m'allonge plusieurs fois, je m'arrête plusieurs fois, je me penche plusieurs fois, je m'allonge plusieurs fois sur le trèfle et je me baisse. Mon regard devient à ce qu'il est.

12.

On the way to college, I lie down. I lie in the grass. I lie down and the grass tends to my feet, my hands. I lie down. I lower myself and my gaze becomes what it is. I lie down and my gaze becomes what it is at the same time as what it was. I lean on the grass and I lie down. I lower myself and lie down several times. I stop several times. I lean several times. I lie down on the clover several times and I lower myself. My gaze becomes what it is.

19.

C'est la première fois que j'en vois un, de trèfle, et j'en vois 1 + 1 + 1 + 1 +... Si je le cueille et le place dans ma main brille. Si je le cueille et le place dans le médaillon que je possède aussi dans la réalité, je le possède. Si je me penche et je m'arrête plusieurs fois, je m'allonge plusieurs fois et je compte les feuilles au trèfle et j'en vois 1 + 1 + 1 + 1 +... À la place de ma main brille le médaillon que je possède aussi, dans la réalité je le possède. C'est toi peut-être ?

19.

It's the first time I've seen one, clover, and I see 1 + 1 + 1 + 1 + ... If I pluck it and put it in my hand shines. If I pluck it and put it in the locket I also possess in reality, I possess it. If I lean and stop several times, I lie down several times and I count the clover's leaves and I see 1 + 1 + 1 + 1 + ... In lieu of my hand, the locket I also possess shines, in reality I possess it. Could it be you?

20.

C'est toi peut-être en plus petit ? Ou bien c'est toi ou pas plus grand que toi. Comme quelque chose s'est peut-être glissé à ma place, quelque chose que j'avais glissé à ma place ou juste à côté de ma place sans savoir au juste où se trouvait ma place. C'est si petit un trèfle à 5, 6, ou même 7 feuilles. Depuis pourtant rien n'a changé, rien ne m'est arrivé de terrible. Et si je le jette ou l'offre à quelqu'un qui le désire, si je le donne à quelqu'un qui le désire et me l'arrache. C'est toi peut-être ?

20.

Could it be you but smaller? Either it's you or no bigger than you. As if something might have slipped in my place, something I had slipped in my place or right next to my place without knowing exactly where my place was. It's so small, a clover of 5, 6, or even 7 leaves. Since then nothing has changed, nothing terrible has happened to me. And if I toss it or offer it to someone who wants it, if I give it to someone who wants it and plucks it from me. Could it be you?

21.

Depuis pourtant rien n'a changé. Rien ne m'est arrivé de terrible, même si parfois je rêve qu'on me l'arrache et je le donne. Mon trèfle à 1 + 1 + 1 + 1 + ... parle vite, si vite, il me dit qu'il est rare, d'une rareté telle qu'il me faudrait l'extraire de quelque chose de plus vaste pour le comparer à ceci que je n'ai pas en rêve, il me faudrait l'extraire de quelque chose de plus vaste pour le comparer à ce que je n'ai pas. Ou, simplement, je le coupe en deux, comme il est évident qu'il coupe toujours tout en deux.

21.

Since then, however, nothing has changed. Nothing terrible has happened to me, even if I dream sometimes that it is plucked and I give it away. My clover of 1 + 1 + 1 + 1 + ... speaks quickly, this quickly. It tells me it's rare, so rare that I would have to extract it from something more vast before comparing it to what my dreams do not have. I would have to extract it from something more vast before comparing it to what I do not have. Or I'd simply cut it in half as it is clear that it always cuts everything in half.

22.

Si je conjugue ces moments hors de moi passés si loin de toi, avec ce loin qui est « je vois » et toi qui es « si loin de moi », plus ces moments-là sont lointains, plus ils existent en dehors de moi, mieux je les vois. Comme parfois je te sens vivante, je te cueille et j'en ai plein les poches. Ce serait une belle idée de remplir nos poches de toutes les présences qu'on aurait connues pour les retrouver. Et quand je marche avec au-devant, toi, quand je marche aveuglément, empéguée dans mon ombre qui est mon projet, aveugle et aveuglée, les papiers collent à ma marche et crépitent au fond de mes poches. Mais moi ça ne me dérange pas, tu sais, quand quelque chose s'échappe de mes poches avec ton rire qui vient vers moi.

22.

If I conjugate the moments outside of me, spent so far from you, with this distance that is "I see" and you who are "so far from me," the more distant these moments are from me, the more they exist outside me, the better I see them. Like at times when I feel you alive, I pluck you and my pockets are full. It would be a great idea to fill our pockets with all the presences we have known to find them again. And when I walk with, ahead, you, when I walk blindly, stuck in my shadow, my project, blind and blinded, papers stick to my stride and crackle deep in my pockets. But, you know, it's not a problem for me when something slips out of my pockets with your laughter coming at me.

23.

Si je conjugue ces moments hors de moi passés si loin de toi, à la fois je les pense si fort, je les cueille si fort et j'en ai plein les poches. Et je marche avec mes poches qui crépitent d'une manière totalement nouvelle. Car dans mes poches il y a des bombes qui sont des sons et à la fois des bombes et des sons et des sons compris dans des sons. Comme parfois je me penche au bord de toi et qu'il est tard, si tard, les sons éclatent une fois pour voir et toutes les fois de chaque fois que l'on marche ensemble, ils éclatent.

23.

If I conjugate the moments outside of me, spent so far from you, I think of them forcefully, I pluck them forcefully and my pockets are full. And I walk with my pockets crackling in a completely new manner. For in my pockets are bombs that are sounds and at the same time bombs and sounds and sounds that include sounds. Like at times I lean on your edge and it's late, too late, sounds split open to see one and every instant in each instance we walk together. They split open.

24.

Pour nous qui ne sommes qu'un instant doués de vie, ce sont de justes sentiments, de tendres sentiments de l'un vers l'autre, tendant si loin de l'autre. La loi est réversible qui dit que deux va de face et un de côté. Alors elle tangue, la possibilité, tant qu'elle est là et comme c'est bon d'être là avec elle, tu t'imagines comme c'est bon, et quel spectacle c'est de la voir, à ce moment-là, en ta vie entière contenue. Mais ce qu'elle ne dit pas, c'est qu'elle est là tout de suite et qu'ainsi de suite elle est à la fois le meilleur et le pire des jougs, comme chaque fois qu'elle veut marcher vers toi et que ta vie s'arrête.

24.

For us, who are nothing but a blessed moment of life, these are valid feelings, feelings of tenderness for each other, stretching so far from the other. The law is reversible and says there are two on the front and one on the side. Then she staggers, the possibility, so long as she's here and as it's good to be here with her. You can see how good it is, and what a sight it is to see her, right now, inside your whole life. But what she doesn't say is that she's right there and as such she is both the best and worst of yokes, like every time she wants to walk toward you and your life stops.

25.

Il n'y a pas de doute possible. Il n'y a pas de doute qui se découpe en plus petites unités. Il n'y a pas de détail que l'on puisse réduire à de plus petites unités parce qu'il n'y a pas de détail moindre. Il n'y a pas de détail hors des faits ni de fait hors des détails. Hormis peut-être des détails, il n'y a que des faits. Il y a ce qui se dit et s'accroche. Il y a ce qui se dit et s'accroche à son immédiat entourage. Il y a de petites perturbations dans l'air qui engloutissent à la fois l'air et les pierres et les recrachent. Il y a ce qui se dit qui est limpide, à condition qu'une source de chaleur le touche. Le moment où les larmes vont couler est le seul moment juste.

25.

There is no possible doubt. There is no doubt that divides into smaller units. There is no detail we could reduce to smaller units because there is no lesser detail. There are neither details other than facts nor facts other than details. There is nothing other than facts, maybe, except for details. There is what is said and what sticks. There is what is said and what sticks to its immediate entourage. There are slight disturbances in the air that swallow both air and rocks and regurgitate them. There is what is said, which is limpid, provided that a source of heat is touching it. The only just moment is the moment when tears flow.

26.

Et si elles coulent, les larmes, même avant qu'elles ne coulent et ne se forment au coin de l'œil, elles dévient à partir de cet œil et roulent le long du cou et le reste du corps. Alors que nous voudrions contenir cette rivière de larmes nous ne le pouvons pas. Il y a de l'abus, dans l'air. Il y a des pensées abrégées de leurs possibilités. Il y a le tir tac-tac des mitraillettes qui dessinent de jolies machines dans le passé. Nous ne ménageons pas nos efforts pour tenir tac-tac dans le ballet mobile, nous nous battons. Parfois nous manquons à nos vivres mais nous nous battons. Et tandis qu'ils débarquent nos vivres, tandis qu'ils versent à terre nos faibles densités et que l'air se retourne, nous nous battons. Et nos larmes n'ont qu'un visage. Elles sont des pierres sur nos joues, comme jamais les pierres ne cesseront de rire des plus petites pierres et de produire à leur tour des pierres de plus en plus petites et isolées, et les larmes de couler avec la régularité des pendules d'eau.

26.

And if they flow, the tears, even before they flow, forming in the corner of an eye, they become part of the eye and trickle down the length of the neck and the rest of the body. Though we'd like to hold back the river of tears, we can't. There is abuse in the air. There are thoughts whose possibilities have been abbreviated. There's the rat-tat-tat of submachine-gun fire drawing pretty machines in the past. We don't spare our efforts to keep rat-tat-tat in the movable ballet—we are fighting. Sometimes we miss our vitals, but we are fighting. And as they unload our vitals, while they pour our feeble solids on the ground and the air comes about, we're fighting. And our tears have but one face. They are rocks on our cheeks, as they'll never stop laughing at the smaller rocks and producing, in turn, smaller and more isolated rocks, and the tears will never stop flowing steadily from pendulums of water.

27.

Il n'y a pas d'effets secondaires, juste des effets de peau. Vous voyez ces maisons, la verdure ? Si vous restez près du buisson, vous voyez le buisson sur le toit de la deuxième maison ? Il ne reste rien là-bas, à part le trou et le camion rempli d'eau. Après la maison, à côté du buisson, il y a le trou. Je l'ai survolé l'autre jour, quand on le survole on voit que tout a disparu. À la fois je veux bien qu'ça disparaisse, c'était pas beau. Regardez à l'intérieur de la maison au moment où le camion va passer sur la parcelle. C'est dans ce bâtiment qu'ils ont fait ça à nous. Ça a chauffé dans l'air. À ma très grosse surprise. À ma grosse tête gonflée d'hélium. À cette enfance aux courroies lâches, à ce qui tremble et s'est jeté sur nous. À cette surface tangible, de contact, préhensible. À ce geste où je te touche. Mon corps est lourd à cause des mille trèfles qui bondissent à l'intérieur. Tu te diffractes mais tu tiens bon. Dans la pénurie des vivres je refais les jours, et je tombe dans une musique autrefois douce. Comme la plus grande des soifs s'est probablement tarie. Ton scintillement n'était pas vain. Avec cette légèreté qui remplit l'air à nouveau. Vite, 5 ou 6 petits bouts de trèfle à moitié coupés dans la bouche.

27.

There are no secondary effects, only the effects of skin. Can you see those houses, the foliage? If you stay close to the brush, can you see the brush on the roof of the second house? There's nothing left there except the hole and the truck full of water. Beyond the house, next to the brush, there's the hole. I glanced at it the other day. When you glance at it you see that everything has disappeared. At the same time, I want it to disappear. It wasn't pretty. Look inside the house when the truck passes the plot of land. It is in this building that they did this to us. It got hot in the air. To my great surprise. To my big head bloated with helium. To this careless childhood, to what trembles and has been thrown on us. To this tangible, seizable point of contact. To this gesture with which I touch you. My body is heavy because there are a thousand clovers bouncing around inside it. You diffract but you hold on. In the shortage of vitals I redo the days and fall into a once pleasant music. As the greatest of thirsts has no doubt run dry. Your scintillation was not useless. With this lightness that replenishes the air again. Quick, 5 or 6 halved clover stems in the mouth.

Décembre

December

1er.

Je me tiens sur les retenues d'une quantité d'eau assez faible. Je ne voudrais l'avoir versée pour rien au monde. Ma voix ne me parvient pas comme une idée fiable. Elle me frappe et si je tombe, dans la chaleur, je m'enfonce dans un silence mat. Je suis de l'eau, brouillant les sons. Et tandis que j'avance dans les couloirs d'un raisonnement truqué, où je glisse plutôt, une ombre s'abat sur ma joue et s'enfouit dans les reliefs où précédemment je portais ma fierté. J'imagine qu'elle s'installe sur mon visage qui se couvre du même effet. Quelque chose s'active en moi qui sommeillais. Je ferme les yeux, je marche, et mes yeux ne sont jamais fermés.

1st.

I stand on the restraints of rather small quantities of water. I wouldn't like to have poured it out for anything in the world. My voice does not come to me like a reliable idea. It hits me, and if I fall in the heat I sink into a matte silence. I am water, warping sounds. And as I advance down the hallways of false reasoning, as I slip, rather, a shadow falls on my cheek and buries itself in the leftovers where I once kept my pride. I imagine it situating itself on my face, covered by the same effect. Something once dormant is activated inside me. I close my eyes, I walk, and my eyes are never closed.

2.

Dehors il y a un espace qui n'est pas habité mais je le veille. Il y a une chaise qui attend. Des chaussures sont posées dans un coin. Les enfants savent lorsqu'il faut jouer désespérément. Je reste à distance de cette idée. J'inverse mes oreilles pour mieux entendre. Mes yeux s'enfoncent dans mon visage et réapparaissent sur l'autre face. Bois le visage, le mange tout. Et le roucoulement de n'importe quel oiseau, dans la mesure où il me parvient, dit simplement « je suis inconsolable » tient lieu ici d'éternité.

2.

Outside there is a space that is uninhabited, but I watch over it. There is a chair waiting. Shoes placed in the corner. Children know when they need to play desperately. I stay away from that idea. I invert my ears to hear better. My eyes sink into my face and resurface on the other face. Drink the face, eat it whole. And the cooing of any bird, in how it comes to me, says simply *I am inconsolable*, here serves as eternity.

3.

Je n'avance pas plus vite. Je me laisse gagner par cette immobilité fortuite. Et si je tombe dans la redite, je chantais ce jour-là seulement pour tromper l'ennui. Sans doute est-il trop tard pour commenter ce geste de défonce, de sorte qu'à la fin de cette page, je vous demanderai pardon.

3.

I move forward no faster. I let this fortuitous immobility win me over. And if I fall into repetition, I was only singing that day to trick tedium. It is no doubt too late to comment on this gesture of registration so that, at the end of the page, I'll beg your pardon.

4.

J'étais cette jeune fille normale. Corps émacié, visage bleui, j'inventais un bateau dont la cale s'étirait sur le port. De la nature autour de moi j'aurais pu dire mon désarroi était grand. Ce que je perçois, à l'arrivée, n'est pas morose. J'étais, dit-elle, déconstruite, la silhouette et le corps s'excluant. J'avais un tee-shirt qui pleurait simplement. De cette indétermination je ne peux concevoir si elle relève d'un ordre plus grand. La voix répète plusieurs fois le phonème de l'oiseau. Je ne dis pas ce mot, mais si je casse la branche, la phrase dure une seconde de plus qu'elle ne dure. Et tandis que je meurs d'envie, j'avance dans le vacarme d'un après-midi débondant ses fruits, ses fanes et ses rosiers muscats. La page après la page établit la suivante. Une théorie veut clore ici. Nous passerons sans embarras.

4.

I was that normal girl. Gaunt body, blue face, I made up a ship whose cargo hold spread into the harbor. Of the nature surrounding me I could have said my disarray was great. What I perceive on arrival is not morose. I was, she said, deconstructed, the silhouette and the body each refusing the other. I had a t-shirt that would only cry. I cannot conceive whether this indeterminacy comes from a higher order. The voice repeats the bird's phoneme several times. I do not say that word but if I break the branch then the sentence lasts one second longer than it lasts. And, although I'm dying to, I move through the racket of an afternoon overflowing with fruit, dead leaves, and muscat rose bushes. The page after the page sets up the next. Here, a theory wants to enclose. We'll pass through without embarrassment.

9.

Nous sommes tenues par une promesse, une norme de motifs, logiques en apparence, visibles à l'agencement des couleurs et à l'imbrication des formes dans le mur. Un jour, le récipient déborde et le chien hurle. On ouvre la porte et dehors les bobines trompent la pellicule. Du reste, tout n'est pas dit. L'aboiement du chien prolonge un sentiment de vide. Se peut-il qu'un regard dépourvu de vitesse reste ainsi tendu dans sa pratique ? L'instant suivant, quelque chose a changé : les blancs sont plus blancs, la chemise a des bleus, des gris, des violets. Le plan du visage compose un lieu indéchiffrable. On dirait que quelque chose s'est produit ou développe ses effets diffractés.

9.

We are bound by a promise, a standard pattern, logical in appearance, visible in an arrangement of colors and interwoven figures in the wall. One day, the vessel brims over and the dog howls. We open the door and the facial expressions outside fool the roll of film. Of the rest, all is not said. The dog's howl prolongs a sense of emptiness. Can it be that a gaze deprived of speed keeps its tension in practice? The next moment—something has changed: the whites are whiter, the shirt has two blues, grays, violets. The flat plane of a face composes an indecipherable location. One could say that something has come to pass or develops its diffracted effects.

15.

Images indistinctes, démêlées du fond. Lieux communs mille fois traversés. Idiomes intacts. On voudrait s'assécher, former autour d'elles un pur esprit de mailles. On laisse les portes entrebâillées. Elles ne changent pas d'aspect avec le temps. Autre découverte : si vous êtes le cœur, il faut rêver les membres. La marque d'une fiction change, un rien superficiel. Maintenant avance, charge ta viande. Travaille-la soigneusement, fût-elle avariée. Avec un papier plié dans la bouche pour dévier ton souffle, tu ne peux pas faire de bruit.

15.

Indistinct images, disentangled from depth. Common locations crossed a thousand times. Intact idioms. We'd like to dry out to form a pure spirit of meshes around them. We leave the doors ajar. Their appearance does not change over time. Another discovery: if you are the heart, the limbs must be dreamt. The mark of fiction changes—a superficial nothing. Move forward now, load up your meat. Work it with care, even if it's rotten. With a piece of paper folded in your mouth, deflecting your breath, you can't make any noise."

22.

La posture est nouvelle pour moi, excellente. Soudain je me sens vivre en nombre illimité. À celle qui se sentirait autrement dépourvue : approche, tente ta chance. Regarde le cœur qui te regarde. Il est cette petite blessure, qu'on écrase avec le pied. Attachement : seul le métier remue.

22.

The position is new for me—excellent. Suddenly I feel alive in unlimited number. To those who feel otherwise deprived: come, try your luck. Look at the heart looking at you. It is a little wound we flatten with a foot. Attachment: only craft moves.

Translator's Afterword

Marie de Quatrebarbes's *The Vitals* is, at least on its surface, a recomposition of a daily journal whose entries run from July to December of an unspecified year. Though not directly stated, it becomes clear that at some point before or during the writing of this journal an irreparable loss has occurred, mauling a hole at the center of the journal writers' consciousness: "I'm no longer there when she leaves me." Avoiding anything resembling a linear narrative to relate this loss, de Quatrebarbes's journal is all the more intimate, exhibiting a deep, messy, and earnest interiority. Here, logos and pathos intersect in flesh more than sense. Instead of a craft of seamlessness in service of a larger quilt, *The Vitals* is all seams, in service of seams. As de Quatrebarbes writes, "there is no detail we could reduce to smaller units because there is no lesser detail."

Within the framework of the journal, lacunae in time become significant as well. The poems/journal entries frequently skip several days at a time. (July 1 through 8 are in regular succession, but then it jumps to July 13, then 19, and then 26, and so forth.) The gaps in the sequence suggest that something is being withheld, that an image of completion hides behind those undocumented days, such that absence looms in the book's very structure. These temporal gaps hold us in the suspension of loss, emphasizing the contours of the time in between. To sketch the experience of grief, de Quatrebarbes's text embodies the task of bearing—bearing weight, bearing loss in the passage of time. What emerges is a coming to awareness of the slow and absurd labor of being someone without the other.

De Quatrebarbes's sentences play out accordingly: phrases come to and fall away in fits and starts, amorphously, with "enough life to decide at another time." Their subjects, objects, actions, and events follow suit. With an uncanny assurance, *The Vitals* confronts us with such unorthodox sentences, each carefully formed: they end on subordinating conjunctions, active and passive voices play opposite day, and prepositional gestures usurp the main clauses. Perhaps most strikingly, subjects and objects interlock, obscuring whether a figure is a person, an hourglass, or a shout from the children's bedroom: "On the tapestry shapes recited dictionary entries I took for images." Syntactic disruption in turn disrupts the order of subjects and objects in space and time, and becomes the focal point of *The Vitals*. Rational meaning falls by the wayside, or, rather, new meanings appear that cannot be made through normative grammar. The book's formal difference (its unfamiliarity) brings about a sensation, an atmosphere, a mood to be felt.

One might say that *The Vitals* is not interested in being a "book." There is only the pretense of character—or is it a figure, or maybe an identity? None of these words wholly work for the people, or relationships, as they play out in this sequence. Character, figure, and identity: these terms depend on definition, and in *The Vitals,* narrative is indefinite. The story (if a singular story is to be found in it) is constantly obscuring its own beginning and end. Moreover, there are neither overarching symbologies nor single clear moments of epiphany. Instead, one gets the immediate impression that the rules of language have been meticulously contorted, building a world suddenly unfamiliar—the experience of a reality forced into flirtation with artifice. When language is set in the contortions that de Quatrebarbes produces in *The Vitals*, what remains to be recognized within it? What does language have if not coherence or definition?

At the very least, without these two, language still has sound. A sentence, an utterance—down to the smallest unit of sound. What might be primarily looked for in *The Vitals* is not coherence but the manipulation of sound as the form coherence takes—everything about *how* coherence registers instead of *why* or *what* it registers. It becomes clear then, that this poetry is not entirely disinterested in coherence or definition. Rather, it is interested in coherence and definition in terms of how they play and can be played with as filters of experience, using the medium of language to deny them and then to see what replenishes the space created by their absence.

It is not a given that *The Vitals* should be placed in a particular "tradition," considering both the diffuse nature of "movements" in contemporary French poetry and this work's indifference toward seeking them out. However, there is a nod to the stark yet at-ease compositions of Dominique Fourcade, particularly in his book-length work *Rose-déclic (Click-rose)*. De Quatrebarbes embellishes a similar unphased, quotidian futility. Stronger still is *The Vitals*' poetic communication with de Quatrebarbes's American counterparts, particularly those associated with the experiments of Language poetry. Traces of the theoretical through-line-turned-praxis of Lyn Hejinian's *My Life*, the sociality and procedural horror of Leslie Scalapino's *way*, and the stamina and playfulness of Bernadette Mayer's *Midwinter's Day* are abundant. De Quatrebarbes' editorial work at Éditions Corti, a Paris-based independent publisher of poetry, underscores this connection: the publisher's Série Américaine includes French translations of American experimentalists such as John Ashbery, Gertrude Stein, Rae Armantrout, Cole Swensen, Claudia Rankine, Keith Waldrop, and the aforementioned Scalapino. A reader of the wide range of poetics these names represent will find kinship in *The Vitals*.

Korean-American poet Myung Mi Kim's approach to both reading and writing illuminates de Quatrebarbes's poetics in

The Vitals. In an interview for *Bayou Magazine,* Kim discusses the relationship of her poetics to her childhood immigration and acquisition of English as a second language:

> As a poet I am constantly thinking about … and exploring modes of relating to and generating language that pluralize sense-making … I've become keenly aware of the constitutive elements of language, how even one phoneme might contribute to/reorient perception. I listen for the event of language—every element, component, scrap, particle—whether graphic, sonic, rhythmic, kinetic—that may be said to contribute to the unfurling of language.*

The Vitals is made of a keen awareness of the elements, components, scraps, and particles of language Kim describes, of de Quatrebarbes's sensitivity to "the event of language" as more than reflective or expressive of experience, but as its own site of experience, its own embodiment. This translation is a document of the necessarily imperfect acquisition and reformulation of the particular French of de Quatrebarbes's *Les vivres.*

---

* Marian Kaufman, "Interview with Myung Mi Kim." *Bayou Magazine.* https://bayoumagazine.org/interview-with-myung-mi-kim/

Acknowledgments

The translator would like to give special thanks to the author of this book for her ear, generosity, her commitment to the translation, and friendship.

Gratitude to the editors of the publications where excerpts of this translation have previously been featured: *Asymptote*, *Denver Quarterly*, *Mercury Firs,* and *Posit*.

Thank you to the Albertine Foundation Translation Fund, and to the Dean's Special Project Grant administered by Columbia University's School of the Arts.

Much appreciation to Rachel Valinsky, Lynn Xu, Allyson Paty, Jo Urtasun, E.R. Pulgar, Ryan Cook, & Nabila Wirakusumah, whose careful reading have been essential, and to Vincent Broqua, Vibeke Madsen, and P.O.L Éditeur. Thanks also to Nora Furlong, Henry Gifford, and Jake Syersak, for their feedback on the translation.

Highest praise for Matvei Yankelevich, Katie Long, and my cherished colleague James Loop, for all the hours spent supporting this book and contemporary poetry in translation.

Merci infiniment à M.C., petit Queteu, Tommy-loo, Lisakimu, et Jamer-amer.

Marie de Quatrebarbes (b. 1984) lives and works in Paris. She has published several books of poetry, including *Voguer* (P.O.L, Winner of the Academie Française's Paul-Verlaine Prize), *Les vivres* (P.O.L), and *Vanités* (Éric Pesty Éditeur), as well as a novel inspired by the life of Aby Warburg, *Aby* (P.O.L). She published *La tête et les cornes*, a poetry and translation review, republished the complete poems of Michel Couturier (*L'ablatif absolu*, La tête et les cornes), and edited an anthology dedicated to contemporary poetry by young French women (*Madame tout le monde*, Le Corridor bleu). Since 2023, she is the co-manager of the French publishing house Éditions Corti.

Aiden Farrell is a poet, translator, editor, and educator. He has published two chapbooks: *lilac lilac* (Portable Press @ Yo-Yo Labs) and *organismalgorithm* (Fence), and his poetry and translations have been featured in *Amygdala*, *Denver Quarterly*, *Spectra Poets*, *Asphalte Magazine*, *Wonder*, and elsewhere. He is the managing editor of Futurepoem, and co-curates the Unnamed reading series with Ryan Cook. *The Vitals* is his debut translation.

This book was set in Adobe Caslon, a revival by Carol Twombley based on eighteenth-century specimen pages by English typefounder William Caslon. Cover design by Andrew Bourne. Typesetting by Don't Look Now. Printed and bound in Lithuania by BALTO Print. Manufactured by Arctic Paper in Sweden, the paper in this book meets EU Ecolabel, Forest Stewardship Council, and Cradle to Cradle certification standards.

 WORLD POETRY

Marie-Noëlle Agniau
The Escapades
tr. Jesse Hover Amar

Nadia Anjuman
Smoke Drifts: Selected Poems
tr. Diana Arterian & Marina Omar

Jean-Paul Auxeméry
Selected Poems
tr. Nathaniel Tarn

Boethius
The Poems from On the Consolation of Philosophy
tr. Peter Glassgold

Maria Borio
Transparencies
tr. Danielle Pieratti

Astrid Cabral
Spotlight on the Word
tr. Alexis Levitin

Jeannette L. Clariond
Goddesses of Water
tr. Samantha Schnee

Jacques Darras
John Scotus Eriugena at Laon
tr. Richard Sieburth

Mario dell'Arco
Day Lasts Forever: Selected Poems
tr. Marc Alan Di Martino

Marie de Quatrebarbes
The Vitals
tr. Aiden Farrell

Olivia Elias
Chaos, Crossing
tr. Kareem James Abu-Zeid

Gastón Fernández
Apparent Breviary
tr. KM Cascia

Jerzy Ficowski
Everything I Don't Know
tr. Jennifer Grotz & Piotr Sommer
PEN AWARD FOR POETRY IN TRANSLATION

Antonio Gamoneda
Book of the Cold
tr. Katherine M. Hedeen & Víctor Rodríguez Núñez

Mireille Gansel
Soul House
tr. Joan Seliger Sidney

Óscar García Sierra
Houston, I'm the problem
tr. Carmen Yus Quintero

Phoebe Giannisi
Homerica
tr. Brian Sneeden

Zuzanna Ginczanka
On Centaurs & Other Poems
tr. Alex Braslavsky

Julien Gracq
Abounding Freedom
tr. Alice Yang

Leeladhar Jagoori
What of the Earth Was Saved
tr. Matt Reeck

Nakedness Is My End: Poems from the Greek Anthology
tr. Edmund Keeley

Birhan Keskin
Earthly Conditions: Selected Poems
tr. Öykü Tekten

Jazra Khaleed
The Light That Burns Us
ed. Karen Van Dyck

Judith Kiros
O
tr. Kira Josefsson

Dimitra Kotoula
The Slow Horizon That Breathes
tr. Maria Nazos

Maria Laina
Hers
tr. Karen Van Dyck

Maria Laina
Rose Fear
tr. Sarah McCann

Perrin Langda
A Few Microseconds on Earth
tr. Pauline Levy Valensi

Anna Malihon
Girl with a Bullet
tr. Olena Jennings

Afrizal Malna
Document Shredding Museum
tr. Daniel Owen

Joyce Mansour
In the Glittering Maw: Selected Poems
tr. C. Francis Fisher

Manuel Maples Arce
Stridentist Poems
tr. KM Cascia

Ennio Moltedo
Night
tr. Marguerite Feitlowitz

Meret Oppenheim
The Loveliest Vowel Empties: Collected Poems
tr. Kathleen Heil

Giovanni Pascoli
Last Dream
tr. Geoffrey Brock
RAIZISS/DE PALCHI TRANSLATION AWARD

Gabriel Pomerand
Saint Ghetto of the Loans
tr. Michael Kasper & Bhamati Viswanathan

Liliana Ponce
Theory of the Voice and Dream
tr. Michael Martin Shea

Rainer Maria Rilke
Where the Paths Do Not Go
tr. Burton Pike

Amelia Rosselli
Document
tr. Roberta Antognini & Deborah Woodard

Elisabeth Rynell
Night Talks
tr. Rika Lesser

Waly Salomão
Border Fare
tr. Maryam Monalisa Gharavi

George Sarantaris
Abyss and Song: Selected Poems
tr. Pria Louka

George Seferis
Book of Exercises II
tr. Jennifer R. Kellogg

Seo Jung Hak
The Cheapest France in Town
tr. Megan Sungyoon

Ahmad Shamlou
Elegies of the Earth: Selected Poems
tr. Niloufar Talebi

Ardengo Soffici
Simultaneities & Lyric Chemisms
tr. Olivia E. Sears

Liesl Ujvary
Good & Safe
tr. Ann Cotten & Anna-Isabella Dinwoodie

Paul Verlaine
Before Wisdom: The Early Poems
tr. Keith Waldrop & K.A. Hays

Witold Wirpsza
Apotheosis of Music
tr. Frank L. Vigoda

Uljana Wolf
kochanie, today i bought bread
tr. Greg Nissan

Ye Lijun
My Mountain Country
tr. Fiona Sze-Lorrain

Verónica Zondek
Cold Fire
tr. Katherine Silver